The Gospel
according to Noah

Judy Johnson

The Gospel According to Noah

All rights reserved. This book is protected under the copyright laws of the United States of America and may not be copied or reprinted for commercial gain or profit.

ISBN: 978-1-60920-040-4

Library of Congress Cataloging-in-Publication Data

Unless otherwise indicated, all Scripture quotations are from the *New International Version* of the Bible.

All other references will be designated in the *Notes* section at the end or designated by abbreviation within the text as follows:

All Scriptures marked NAS are from the *New American Standard Bible.*

All Scriptures marked KJV are from the *King James Version.*

All Scriptures marked NKJ are from the *New King James.*

All Scriptures marked LB are from *The Living Bible.*

The author has included all parentheses, italics and bold-faced words for emphasis or explanation. Satan or devil are not capitalized, unless the first word of a sentence, so as not to give recognition to the archenemy. Other words, pertaining to Salvation, Heaven, God, attributes such as Mercy and Grace, His Church, or their pronouns, are capitalized contrary to the rules of grammar, in order to acknowledge their special importance to the message and the *things of God* that are being mentioned.

API
Ajoyin Publishing, Inc.
P.O. 342
Three Rivers, MI 49093

www.ajoyin.com

Please direct your inquiries to admin@ajoyin.com

Contents

Prologue · 1

Introduction · 4

Day 1 *Mathew 24:37–39* · 8

Day 2 *Genesis 6:5* · 10

Day 3 *Genesis 5:29 KJV* · 12

Day 4 *Hebrews 11:7 NKJ* · 14

Day 5 *Genesis 6:9* · 16

Day 6 *Ephesians 5:1 & 2 LB* · 18

Day 7 *Hebrews 4:16* · 20

Day 8 *Genesis 6:8 NKJ* · 22

Day 9 *Exodus 33:12 NKJ* · 24

Day 10 *Matthew 11:28 & 29* · 26

Day 11 *Hebrews 4:16* · 28

Day 12 *Genesis 6:14 NKJ* · 30

Day 13 *Genesis 6:18* · 32

Day 14 *Hebrews 11:7 NKJ* · 34

Day 15 *Exodus 19:4* · 36

Day 16 *Genesis 7:11 NKJ* · 38

Day 17 *Psalm 42:7* · 40

Day 18 *Isaiah 11:9 & 10* · 42

Day 19 *Genesis 7:17 NKJ* · 44

Day 20 *Genesis 1:2 KJV* · 46

Day 21 *Genesis 7:17* · 48

Day 22 *Genesis 8:6 & 7 NKJ* · 50

Day 23 *Genesis 8:9 KJV* · 52

Day 24 *I Peter 1:3 & 4 NKJ* · 54

Day 25 *Genesis 8:9* · 56

Day 26 *Song of Solomon 5:12 LB* · 58

Day 27 *Genesis 8:13* · 60

Day 28 *Genesis 8:20* · 62

Day 29 *John 16:33* · 64

Day 30 *John 16:33 LB* · 66

Day 31 *Genesis 8:9 LB* · 68

Notes · 70

Addendum · 76

Prayer · 78

Prologue

A word about this first book in a series:

On September 6, 1997, **God spoke to me, to begin writing.** He put these devotional studies in my heart and gave me the name: *"Dew Drops In the Morning Sun."* This name is based on Exodus 16:13–15 NAS:

> *"In the morning there was a layer of dew around the camp. When the layer of dew evaporated, behold, on the surface of the wilderness there was a fine-like thing, fine as the frost on the ground. When the sons of Israel saw it, they said to one another, 'What is it?' For they did not know what it was. And Moses said to them, 'It is **bread** which the LORD has given you to eat.' This is **what the LORD has commanded,** 'Gather of it every man as much as he should eat.'"*

The same question has been asked of me, about these devotionals, as was asked about the manna, in the wilderness: "What is it?" As God gave Israel their daily provision of physical food, to sustain their bodies, so God gives us a daily supply of spiritual food. Jesus said, of Himself, in John 6:35; 57 NAS:

> *"I am the **bread of life**…As the Living Father sent Me, and I live because of the Father, so He who eats Me, he also shall live because of Me."*

Moses, also, brought witness to this need for the *Living Bread,* when in Deuteronomy 8:3, he testified:

"And He humbled you and let you be hungry, and fed you with manna which you did not know, nor did your fathers know, that He might make your understand that man does not live by bread alone, but man lives by everything that proceeds out of the mouth of the LORD" (NAS).

We are to live by God's *proceeding words,* that is, the words He speaks to us, *daily.* The manna in the wilderness was **light,** as the morning dew. Just, so, the Spirit comes, *gently* and as *lightly* as a dove, to deposit little nuggets of Truth in our hearts. We must learn to recognize His Voice, so we may gather our daily supply.

This is how these studies developed: They came in the early morning hours, as **gently as the dew.** I, then, gathered the little nuggets of Truth together, to form what you will read, on the following pages.

Eat daily of God's Living Bread,
so you'll be like those gone on, ahead,
who grew up in Jesus, fearless and strong:
doing the right; shunning the wrong;
able to stand, when in the test;
desiring, only, God's very best!

Eat daily of God's Word and, so, you'll see
the devil's hordes, having to flee:
for they don't like hanging around
fearless ones, proved pure, strong, and sound:
refusing to bend; standing their ground;
wanting in Jesus, alone, to be found.

As you eat, daily, of God's Living Bread
you will, always, be well fed,
and the Promise Land you'll, surely, possess
and come to inherit Eternal Rest.
You will stand among the **most blest,**
because **you desired His very best!**

"For precept must be upon precept,
line upon line, line upon line,
here a little, there a little."

Isaiah 28:10 NKJ

INTRODUCTION

The night Jesus was betrayed, He was not thinking of Himself, as He ministered to His disciples, washed their feet, and served them communion.

Jesus entered Gethsemane to become the **wine,** in the **winepress** of God. He, experientially, became that which He was serving His disciples.

Gethsemane means **oil-press.** It refers to the press where the olives, grown in that garden, were placed, in order to convert them from fruit to oil.

In Gethsemane, Jesus was *squeezed* in His inner man, until great drops of blood broke through his skin, as sweat. He said, "My soul is **exceedingly sorrowful,** even to death." Yet, He did not *isolate* Himself, but had three of his disciples come with Him, as He began to be **troubled** and very **distressed** (Mark 14:33 & 34). He needed and desired their *fellowship in His sufferings,* in this most difficult hour!

As Jesus hung on the cross, His thoughts were upon His mother (John 19:26–27). He endured the cross by thinking about the Church, for whom He died (Hebrews 12:2). Jesus, always, put others first, even in His death!

Yet, we see the Church, much like the sleepy disciples (Mark 14:37 & 38). Isaiah 59:15 & 16 describes what Jesus might have felt, as He looked on them, asleep and oblivious of His need and pending fate:

"So truth fails, and he who departs from evil makes himself a prey. Then the LORD saw it, and it displeased Him that there was no justice. He saw that there was no man, and wondered that there was no intercessor."

Where were Jesus' intercessors, in His darkest hour? Fast asleep! Where are His intercessors, in this darkened hour? Hopefully, unlike Peter, James and John, we are not sleeping!

But, are we *willing* to enter Gethsemane, with our Lord? Are we *ready* to share in the fellowship of His sufferings, to each bear our cross? Are we *willing* to do our part to reach a world, for whom Jesus died? Are we *ready* to intercede?

Or, will the LORD, once again, have to say: "I saw that there was no man, and wondered that there was no intercessor."

God is looking for those sensitive to His heart, who will come close enough, to *feel* what He is feeling. He is calling those into Gethsemane with Him, who will *share* in His Heart of love and compassion, for a lost world that is perishing, unless we intercede.

There are many ways to intercede, the primary being prayer. However, Noah interceded for ours and his generation, when in fear, he moved in obedience to build an ark, to the saving of his household, his generation, and all that followed.

Jesus obeyed His Father and said, "Not My will, but Yours be done," as He interceded for the Salvation of all souls, living from the time of Adam, till the end of time.

You may be the, only, intercessor God is able to find and use, in your situation. Be found faithful and obedient, where God has placed you. And, whatever He says for you to do, **do it!** (John 2:5)

Noah, not only, obeyed God as He built the ark, as God commanded, but, refusing to *isolate* from the evil surrounding him, Noah *preached righteousness,* by life and word.

As Noah and Jesus gave of themselves, to be intercessors to their generations, may God find us, so, doing in ours. May our lives make a difference, so that because we *lived,* that is, *lived for Jesus,* others do not perish. Be a **history maker!**

This is the Gospel, according to Noah!

Day 1

As it was in the days of Noah, so it will be at the coming of the Son of Man. For in the days before the flood, people were eating and drinking, marrying and giving in marriage, up to the day Noah entered the ark; and they knew nothing about what would happen until the flood came and took them all away. That is how it will be at the coming of the Son of Man.

The Days of Noah

We are in **the days of Noah,** foretold by the LORD. The disciples, like us, were, always, hoping for a word, vision or revelation, that would enable them to peer into what is coming on the earth. Jesus said the earth would, once again, be marked by **great corruption,** just before His return.

Before the flood, the people were spiritually and **morally corrupt.** *After* the flood, their dead bodies were strewn upon the waters, **physically decayed** and **corrupted.** Spiritual death leads to physical death.

When I was a child, we would sometimes hear the expression, "That kid is **rotten!**" What was meant was, *"Morally,* that child is *corrupted!"* The word **corruption** in Genesis 6, also, means *decayed* or *rotten!*[1]

Ephesians 2: 1 & 2 speaks of mankind's unsaved condition:[2]

> *"You hath He quickened **who were dead** in trespasses and sins; Wherein in time past you walked according to the course of this world, according to the prince of the power of the air, the spirit that now works in the children of disobedience."*

MATHEW 24:37–39

When we get saved, the Spirit of God *quickens* us out of **death, decay,** and **corruption,** *spiritually,* as I Peter 1:3 & 4, further, tell us:

> *"Praise be the God and Father of our Lord Jesus Christ! In His great mercy He has given us new birth into a living hope through the resurrection of Jesus Christ from the dead, to an inheritance that can never **perish, spoil,** or **fade away**—kept in heaven for you…"*

As God's fruit,
we have been **preserved,**
so as not to **spoil!!**

Day 2

*The LORD saw how **great man's wickedness** on the earth had become, and that every inclination of the thoughts of his heart was **only evil all the time.***

A CREATION TURNED SOUR

Noah lived in a world **filled with great wickedness. Wickedness,** basically, means that which is *bad* or *evil.*[1] It derives from another root word, meaning *to spoil* or be *good for nothing.*[2]

If that were not enough, God goes on to inform us, their *every thought* was, *continuously,* evil. The word **evil** means their thoughts were **unable to come up to good standards that benefit.**[3]

God declared His original creation **good** and **productive.**[4] In Noah's day, that creation had, now, become **evil, unproductive,** and **unbeneficial.**

The corruption multiplied, until the earth was *filled with violence.*[5] **Violence** could, also, mean:[6]

- Wrong
- Cruel
- Unrighteous
- Dealing Violently
- Unjust
- Doing Damage
- False

One word can sum up all these words, used to describe the *wicked,* in Noah's day: **Abusers!** It could, also, be an apt description of the wicked of our day.

GENESIS 6:5

We, often, hear of fathers *abusing* children, husbands *beating* wives, children *abusing* parents, and perverts *stalking, kidnapping* and *violating* young women and children, all of which are on the increase.

The wickedness was very great, *great* meaning to **abound** or to be **abundant**. It describes anything that is *manifold* and, *exceedingly, great* in *number* or *degree.*[7]

The *extent,* or *degree* of wickedness, had reached such proportions that God found it necessary to destroy everything. Otherwise, no one would have been saved, but all mankind, from all generations, would have been condemned to hell.

However, God found **one righteous man,** Noah, through whom He could continue the human race, until a Savior could come, bringing salvation to all.

Wickedness does not stand still,
but **increases,** till all earth it fills.

It will **infiltrate** all mankind,
if, to its evil, we resign.

Its design is to **corrupt,**
GOD'S GOOD PLAN to **disrupt!**

Day 3

And he called his name Noah, saying, "This same shall comfort us concerning our work and toil of the ground which the LORD hath cursed."

The Comforter Is Come

Lamech named his son Noah, because, he said, "This same shall **comfort us."** God used Noah's name, to predict that he would be a *source of comfort,* for those living in his day.

There is a sense, in which Noah was a *comfort* to God and us, as well. Without Noah, the entire world, of his time, would have perished. In addition, every person that lived, from Adam until Noah's time, would have been lost, eternally.

Because all flesh had corrupted their way on the earth, God searched for a righteous man, through whom He could continue the human race and bring forth a Savior, in time.[1] Noah was His man!

Noah moved with fear and prepared an ark, to the **saving of his household.**[2] By saving *his household,* Noah saved an, even, *greater household.* We **all** were on that boat, with him.

Without Noah, God's *eternal purpose,* for all mankind, would have been lost. This truth should cause us to reflect upon Jesus, as our Savior. The hope and help of *all humanity* and God's eternal purpose rested upon Him, as He hung on the Cross. Once again, **we were there** on that cross, with Him. He is the door into the eternal, Ark of Safety, **we must enter.**

GENESIS 5:29 KJV

As in Noah's day, so today: whosoever wills may come. One has to wonder why animals heard the voice and wooing of God to come into the ark, while none, but Noah and his household, entered.

God spoke in times past, *by his prophets*, such as Noah. The people of his day are a warning, by example, to us: of the **grave necessity** and **deadly seriousness** of our **receiving** *God's messenger*. All those, who did not heed Noah's message, **perished**.

Today, God is speaking through His Son. He stands AT THE DOOR, *urging* whosoever will **to enter** His Great Salvation.[3] Those who **ignore** His Voice **will not escape** the coming judgment. Once, the door is closed, it will be **eternally, too, late!**

God's great, eternal plan
lay in the hands of **one**
obedient man;

For such vessels
He is looking, still,
who will fulfill His very will,
so Heaven's portals can be filled.

Day 4

*By faith Noah, being divinely warned of things not yet seen, **moved
with Godly fear,** prepared an ark for the saving of his household, by
which he condemned the world and became heir of the righteousness
which is according to faith.*

MOVED TO ACTION

God had need of **one righteous man,** through whom He could
save the existing world and preserve His eternal plan. Noah was
that man!

Upon hearing God's warning of coming judgment, Noah was
moved with Godly fear. His Godly fear moved him *to prepare an
ark.*

It is one thing to fear. Godly fear, however, will **move one to action
and obedience,** as Noah. This Godly kind of fear will *not cause one
to flee from God,* as we saw Adam do, when hearing God's Voice in
the garden.

Instead, Noah **did all** that God had **commanded** him, and, in so
doing, *made preparation* for the salvation of his entire household.[1]
God's purpose is that none perish.[2]

While it is God that brings about His eternal purposes, there must,
also, be **our heart's response of obedience.** Without *our part,* something of God's eternal plan *will perish.*

This was not the *only* time that God's eternal plan hinged on *the
obedience of one.* Whenever a situation was *at its worst,* God, often,
found that **one,** through whom He could **bring a mighty deliverance:**

HEBREWS 11:7 NKJ

- When the **famine** was *at its worst,* God brought forth **Joseph;**

- When the **affliction** of the Hebrews, in Egypt, was at its worst, God sent **Moses;**

- When the **oppression** of the Midianites was *at its worst,* God raised up **Gideon;**

- When the **sin of Nineveh** was *at its worst,* God commissioned **Jonah;**

- When the **world** was *its darkest,* God sent forth **His Son** into the world!

It is a fearful thing
to contemplate,
that on me rides
someone's **eternal fate;**

that if His call *I disobey,*
the boat for them
may be **too late!**

Day 5

Noah was a righteous man, blameless among the people of his time, and he walked with God.

A Pleasurable People

The **Grace of God** that brings salvation *appeared to all men*, according to Titus 2:11. This Grace appeared as far back as Noah's day, for Noah **"found Grace** in the eyes of the LORD."*[1]*

Noah was a *righteous man*, who *walked with God*. His **walk of Grace** was a stark *contrast*, to what, else, God *saw*, for...

> "God saw the **extent of human wickedness**, that the trend and direction of men's lives were **only towards evil**."*[2]*

Therefore, God's heart was **filled with pain!***[3]* Yes, God can **feel pain.** He speaks, often, of that which brings Him pain. He, also, speaks of what brings Him **pleasure.** For example, in Titus 2:14, God reveals His purpose for redemption:

> "to redeem us from all wickedness and to purify for Himself a people that are His very own, eager to do what is good."

His purpose is:

- **To redeem** us from wickedness, and
- **To purify** us, especially, for Himself

God wants a people, who will **bring Him pleasure,** and, with whom, He may **have fellowship.** In other words, **God wants children,** of His very own, who enjoy doing what **brings Him joy.**

GENESIS 6:9

God wants a God-fearing people, who will stand alone, even, when others are very godless. If Noah could walk with God, amongst the evildoers of his day, shouldn't we the more?

We are *all called* to be **a people of His very own,** eager to do His will. If so, then, may each one of us *freely receive this Grace* of God that appeared unto all men. It is a **free gift.** It is **Grace!**

My sacrificial, love walk
will be a **sweet perfume**
that will bring **joy to the**
heart of God, continuously!

Day 6

Follow God's example in everything you do, just as a much loved child imitates his father. Be full of love for others; following the example of Christ who loved you and gave Himself to God as a sacrifice to take away your sins. And God was pleased, for Christ's love for you was like sweet perfume to Him.

LOVE WALKING

Jesus offered Himself, as a **sweet-smelling perfume,** for us. Therefore, we are to:

"...walk in love, as Christ also has loved us..."[1]

The book of Ephesians tells us to **follow God** by *walking* in a *particular manner*...so, as to **imitate Christ:**

- Walk in **forgiveness**[2]
- Walk in **love,** as Christ loved[3]
- Walk in **light**[4]
- Walk in **wisdom,** as to God's will[5]
- Walk in your **calling,** worthily[6]
- Walk in **prudence** (circumspectly), and[7]
- Walk in a **renewed mind**[8]

Noah's life was a **contrast** to those on the earth, in his day, because he *walked with God.* Therefore, he was a *righteous, blameless* man, among the people of his time.

We, too, can **walk, so as to set an example** others can follow, as we follow Christ. Then, our lives in turn, like Jesus', will **be a sweet-smelling perfume:**

Ephesians 5:1 & 2 LB

*"Wherever we go, He uses us to tell others about the Lord and to spread the Gospel like a **sweet perfume**. As far as God is concerned, there is a **sweet, wholesome fragrance** in our lives. It is the **fragrance of Christ** within us, an aroma to both the saved and the unsaved all around us."*

2 Corinthians 2:14 &15 LB

If in **God's Family**
I claim to be,
my character should reflect
His **Family Tree!**

Day 7

*Let us then approach the Throne of Grace with confidence, so that we may receive Mercy and find **Grace to help us** in our time of need.*

GRACE TO MAKE IT

This is the time of the **favor** of the LORD: the time of the LORD's Grace to His Church. In Luke 4:18–19, Jesus identified Himself as the One spoken of, by the prophet Isaiah, as He read from Isaiah 61:1 & 2:

> *"The Spirit of the Sovereign LORD is on Me, because the LORD has anointed Me to preach Good News to the poor. He has sent Me to bind up the broken-hearted, to proclaim freedom for the captives and release from darkness for the prisoners, to proclaim the year of the LORD's favor."*

Without God's Grace, we cannot make it. Grace is how we are to experience these benefits.

John 1:16 & 17 give us the **source** of this Grace:[1]

> *"And of His fullness we have all received, and Grace for Grace. For the law was given through Moses, but **Grace and Truth** came through Jesus Christ."*

- Grace provides **what we need.**
- Truth **sets us free.**[2]

Hebrews 4:16

When we *believe* and *receive* the provision of Grace, the Truth of that revelation will **set us free of**:

- Poverty
- Brokenness
- Bondage, and
- Oppression

At the Throne of Grace, the place of *divine transaction,* we can **exchange** our curses for His benefits.

Noah *looked into the eyes* of the LORD and found Grace! In his time of need, Noah **drank** of **the Grace revealed** in the heart of God! I, too, can *look into His eyes* and heart, and **drink deeply** of His Mercy, and find Grace to aid me in the fight.

Look into the *dove eyes* of the Spirit of Grace!

Have a drink:

Drink of Me
and you will see,
there is **abundant Grace**
for every need!

Day 8

But Noah found Grace in the eyes of the LORD.

A GRACIOUS LOOK

Noah **looked into the eyes of the Lord** and **found Grace.** The Hebrew word for *Grace* means:[1]

- favor, grace, graciousness
- kindness
- beauty, attractiveness, loveliness
- pleasantness, charm
- affectionate regard

It comes from another root word, which means:[2]

- to be *gracious* or *merciful*
- to be *compassionate,*
- to be *favorably inclined*

Noah had to get *close enough* to have **a face-to-face, eye-to-eye** encounter with God. God **looked upon** Noah **graciously,** with mercy and favor, while Noah **looked upon** God and saw His *beauty, graciousness* and *kindness* toward his need.

In other words, the *"seeing"* was in *both directions.* There was an *exchange* and *interaction* between God and Noah. Noah *knew* God and God *knew* Noah. They had a **relationship, together.**

There is another time in the Bible, when God **looked graciously, upon** someone: Moses.

Genesis 6:8 NKJ

God said to Moses,[3]

"*I know you by name, and you have also **found Grace** in My sight.*"

The question is does God *know you by name?* Do you *know Him,* **face to face?** If so, your life will **show it!**

"*God's solid foundation stands firm, sealed with this inscription: '**The Lord knows those who are His**.' And, 'Everyone who confesses the name of the Lord **must turn away from wickedness**.'*"

2 Timothy 2:19

If the Lord
you do claim,
your character must
reflect His name!

Day 9

I know you by name, and you have also found Grace in my sight.

A DIVINE ENCOUNTER

It is said of both, Noah and Moses, they **"found Grace"** in God's **eyes**. Moses went a step further and asked to **see His Glory**. God's response was,

> *"I will make all My goodness pass before you, and I will pro-*
> *claim the name of the LORD before you. I will be gracious to*
> *whom I will be gracious, and I will have compassion on whom*
> *I will have compassion."*

Exodus 33:19 NKJ

So, God put Moses in a cleft of the rock and **proclaimed His name** before him:

> *"And the LORD passed before him and proclaimed,*
>
> *'The LORD, the LORD God, merciful and gracious, long-suffer-*
> *ing and abounding in goodness and truth, keeping mercy for*
> *thousands, forgiving iniquity and transgression and sin, by no*
> *means clearing the guilty, visiting the iniquity of the fathers*
> *upon the children and the children's children to the third and*
> *the fourth generation.'"*

Exodus 34:6 & 7

The result was Moses bowed his head and **worshiped.**[1] Moses *saw* **God's Glory** and Noah *saw* **God's Graciousness**.

Exodus 33:12 NKJ

God has, also, made a way for everyone of us *to find Grace in His sight.* There is *an appointed place* of **divine encounter,** where God can meet whatever *need* you and I are facing, at any given time. **God invites us to this place:**[2]

> *"Let us therefore come boldly to the Throne of Grace, that we may obtain Mercy and find Grace to help in time of need."*

I'll not moan and groan,
but **come, boldly, to the Throne,**
and lay prostrate at Your feet,
so **Your Grace, my need can meet!**

Day 10

*Come to Me, all you who are weary and burdened and **I will give you
rest**. Take My yoke upon you and **learn from Me**, for I am gentle and
humble in heart, and **you will find rest** for your souls.*

A Closer Look

Jesus promises:

- **rest,** in exchange **for our coming,** and
- **rest,** in exchange **for our learning.**

Rest is one of those *needful* things, we are invited to come and
receive, by means of His Grace.[1]

Jesus says, "**Learn from Me:** for, I am gentle and humble in heart."
The words *gentle* and *humble* give us a small glimpse of His Glory.

Much like Moses, we can glimpse a measure of God's Glory, when
He passes **His name,** or **the revelation of His character,** before the
eyes of our understanding.[2] Then, we will know Him in a deeper,
more intimate way, through the Excellency of His Name.

We need to sit and learn at His feet, just as His disciples, who
walked with Him, daily, and Mary, who chose the better thing,
which cannot be taken from her. Mary longed to *know Him, fully,*
so that is where she sat, worshiping and seeking His Glory.[3] Like
Moses, she *knew* who He was and wanted **more.**

The closer you get to Him, the hungrier you will be, for **more of
Him.** Moses, who had spent numerous 40-day encounters on
Mount Sinai, with God in His Glory, still, cried out for more.[4]

MATTHEW 11:28 & 29

Jesus came down to earth to **give us a closer look**.[5] The disciples and Mary were privileged to see the Glory of God, *in the face of Jesus*, whom Moses longed to see.

John, therefore, testified:

> "...*I myself have seen Him with my own eyes and listened to Him speak. I have touched Him with my own hands...He was with the Father and then was **shown to us**.*"

> *I John 1:1 & 2 LB*

Moses' longing, for a glimpse of God's Glory, was fulfilled. One day, he appeared with Elijah, on a high mountain, where Jesus was transfigured.[6] We, too, are destined to **see** God's Glory, if we, only, **believe!**[7]

Don't let what
you **cannot see**,
destroy the joy
of what you **believe!**

Day 11

*Let us then **approach** the Throne of Grace **with confidence**, so that we may receive Mercy and find Grace to help us in our time of need.*

Seek and Find

We are challenged, in Matthew 7:7, to **ask, seek,** and **knock.** The promise is:

> *"For everyone who asks **receives**; he who seeks **finds**, and to him who knocks, the **door** will be **opened**."*

Grace is one of those things we are to **seek** and **find**, according to Hebrews 4:16. The fact we are to **approach, confidently,** assures us that it is meant that we **find.** For, Matthew 7:9–11 goes on, to say:

> *"Which of you, if his son asks for bread will give him a stone? Or if he asks a fish, will he give him a snake? If you then, though you are evil, know how to give good gifts to your children, how much more (that is Grace!) will your Father in Heaven give **good gifts to those who ask Him!**"*

Note, in this illustration, that the Lord used the example of a son *asking* for bread and fish. You may recall that it was the Lord, Himself, that fed the hungry multitude on the mountainside, with bread and fish, from a little boy's lunch.[1]

Jesus would not send them away famished, lest some should faint on the way. Instead, His shepherd's heart had compassion on them. He desired to meet their need, whether *asked or not*.[2]

Hebrews 4:16

We are **guaranteed help** in our personal times of lack, if we come, *petitioning* His Throne.[3] Do we need to, ever, question His willingness to provide, or doubt His compassion toward our need?

Notice the extent of God's provision:

> *"God is able to make all Grace abound to you, so that in all things at all times, **having all that you need**, you will abound in every good work."*
>
> *2 Corinthians 9:8*

It is all received through Grace. Jesus has provided all things for us, through His sacrificial death.

All I need came,
through the Tree,
where Jesus died,
to set me free.

By His Grace
I, now, receive
His abounding sufficiency.

Day 12

Make yourself an ark of gopher-wood; make room in the ark, and cover it inside and outside with pitch.

COVERED THRICE

God told Noah to make an ark of gopher-wood. *Gopher* means **covered** and **pitch-wood.** It also means **to house in.**[1]

The wooden planks, comprising the ark, were to be **covered inside** and **outside with pitch,** to make the ark watertight. A Hebrew derivative, of the word *pitch,* can be translated **camphire, ransom, satisfaction,** or **a redemption price.**[2] Its basic meaning is **cover,** and specifically, **bitumen, coating, Henna,** and **dyeing.**[3]

Henna is used to describe *the Beloved,* in The Song of Solomon. Orientals used the henna plant, to dye the soles of their feet, a *reddish orange.*[4]

The word **cover,** in Genesis 6:14, also, means **to make atonement** or **reconciliation, to pacify, to clear, purge** or **cleanse.** A close derivative, **kippur,** is used in reference to **Yom Kippur,** *the Day of Atonement.*[5]

All this points to the One, who is **our Ark, our covering, atonement, redemption price, ransom, and the satisfaction for our sins,** and **our Beloved.** Our Lord Jesus provided protection, *to insulate* us from the angry waves of God's wrath. His blood was the red orange pitch that dyed two planks of wood, to which He was nailed. We are **sealed within** and **without** by that blood atonement.

Genesis 6:14 NKJ

Just as, *gopher* means *to house in,* Jesus has gone to **prepare a place** of many rooms, **to house in** all those entering in by faith and obedience, to the saving work of the cross.[6]

There was a *third covering,* besides the wood and pitch: In Genesis 8:13, "Noah *removed the covering* of the ark and looked, and indeed...the ground was dry."[7]

This *covering* refers to *weatherboarding.*[8] It comes from a root meaning **to conceal, to cover sin, to wrap oneself up, to forgive.**[9] It was used of the pillars of fire and cloud, whose *covering* protected from the elements. An outer *covering* of *red* badger skins served to protect the Tabernacle.

This *outer covering* over Noah's ark was protection from the elements, as well. Symbolically, it **wrapped up** the ark, and those inside, **in God's forgiveness!**

COVERED without;
COVERED within;
COVERED with blood:
a COVERING for sin;

the redemption price:
His sacrifice;
COVERED by *wood,*
pitch and *blood,*
He COVERED me thrice!

Day 13

But I will establish my Covenant with you, and you will enter the ark—

From Confinement to Enlargement

An ark may seem like a place of *restriction* and *confinement,* where we are **shut in** and **separated,** especially, when the door is closed! But, when the door is opened, again, and we emerge, it is to a **beautiful place,** a **sanctified** and **enlarged place.**

The ark is **a place of protection** in the storm. The waters are like a fiery, trial experience that brings you into **an enlarged place:**

> *"O, bless our God, ye people, and make the voice of His praise to be heard: which holdeth our soul in life, and suffereth not our feet to be moved. For thou, O God, hast tried us, as silver is tried. Thou broughtest us into the net; thou laidest affliction upon our loins. Thou hast caused men to ride over our heads; we went through fire and through water; but **thou broughtest us out into a wealthy place.**"*
>
> *Psalms 66:8–12 KJV*

This experience is, further, described by the Living Bible, in Isaiah 43:1 & 2:

> *"But now the LORD who created you…says, 'Don't be afraid, for I have ransomed you; I have called you by name; you are mine. When you go through deep waters and great trouble, I will be with you. When you go through rivers of difficulty, you will not drown! When you walk through the fire of opposition, you will not be burned up—the flames will not consume you.'"*

Genesis 6:18

When you are going **through a fire or water experience,** that very crisis will **shut you in** to God and **shut out** the world.

A glorious wonder, God performs,
as your image, He transforms:

Cocoon, then, turns to butterfly,
as lowly worm takes to the sky,
to emerge from all confines,
as the old life, it, soon, resigns.

You, too, can mount up, in the sky,
but to the old life, you, first, must die.
In Him, alone, come to abide,
so, in His fullness, you reside.

God's power to others will, then, be known
as works of wisdom, in you, are shown.
So, do not wrest what, now, confines,
But, to that new life, the old resign!

Day 14

By faith Noah, being divinely warned of God of things not yet seen, moved with Godly fear, prepared an ark to the saving of his household; by which he condemned the world and became heir of the righteousness which is according to faith.

FROM DEATH UNTO LIFE

Noah "moved with Godly fear and prepared an ark to the saving of his household." The ark was a place of **safety** and **protection**. At the same time, it became a place of **restriction** and **confinement**.

The ark was, also, a place of **isolation** and **insulation**, and one of **separation**. It *separated* Noah and his family, *from* the floodwaters, *unto* their God.

When the door closed, they were *locked in,* to the **Presence of His Protection**. Being *enclosed*, within the ark, was similar to the experience of Israel, crossing the Red Sea. There, the cloud led them.

The cloud was **light** to the Israelites, while at the same time a **wall of separation** and **darkness** to the Egyptians. Therefore, its Presence served to **isolate** the Israelites from the Egyptians and, thereby, **insulate** them from their enemy and the elements.

The cloud, also, pictures the Gospel of Christ, which is **light and life** to one, while, at the same time, **darkness and death** to those who reject it:

HEBREWS 11:7 NKJ

"For we are to God the aroma of Christ among those who are being saved and those who are perishing. To the one we are the smell of death; to the other, the fragrance of life."

2 Corinthians 2:15 & 16

Going into the ark and coming out; going into the Red Sea, to emerge on the other side; and going down into Jordan, to cross into the Promised Land, all speak of a **death to life experience.** It can be pictured by a worm entering a *restricted, isolated,* and *insulated* **place of confinement,** called a **cocoon,** only to emerge into a *new realm of life,* as a beautiful butterfly, *on the other side.*

When we go through the fire and waters, and affliction is laid on our loins, like a worm in a cocoon, we are being placed into **a protective place,** until we can be brought unto **a wealthy place,** to emerge *transformed!*[1]

If, into a **wealthy place,**
I would come,
to a **death unto life** experience
I must succumb!

Day 15

*You yourselves have seen what I did to Egypt, and how I carried you on eagles' wings and **brought you to Myself**.*

On Eagle Wings

To be *brought unto God* by Himself, personally, is to be brought **unto a wealthy place**.[1] Another version translates wealthy place as **rich fulfillment:**[2]

> *"You have caused men to ride over our head; we went through fire and through water; but You brought us out to **rich fulfillment**."*

It refers to a place of **satisfaction:** a place where one's **cup is running over**.[3] The Hebrew origin of **wealthy place** pictures one, who is athirst, being *saturated and soaked* with water, until, **abundantly, satisfied**.[4]

Noah, in the ark, was in a place of *God's Presence* and *protection:* a place of **isolation and insulation** from the storm. Similarly, when the three Hebrew children were in the fiery furnace, heated seven times hotter, God had *isolated* and *insulated* them *from all hurt*. Upon their bodies, the fire had no power.

In the midst of a violent storm, the disciples were **cocooned in the ark of God's Presence**. Though faithless and fearful, *with Jesus aboard*, they were perfectly safe, nevertheless. With Jesus aboard, we, too, will be safe and secure. In the ark of His Presence, **rest**, **peace** and **calm** will follow our every storm.

Exodus 19:4

The storms of life are *necessary* to deal with our enemies. When Jesus stepped out of the boat with his disciples, after the storm, the demons on the other side, immediately, *cried out with fear.* They knew they were about to be *cast out.* Some things will, also, be *cast out,* when we go through storms.

God bore Israel on eagle's wings, as they came through the Red Sea and journeyed on, through the wilderness. *He brought them unto Himself.*

We tend to see, only, the storm that is raging around us. But, the eagle does not fly **through** the storm, nor fight it. He uses his strength, to soar upward, till he flies **over.** God, like that eagle, is, also, carrying us **up** and **over** and **unto Himself!**

God will lift you up
and bring you out,
unto a wealthy place to sprout;

So, don't try
to fight the storm,
but, to His will,
your life conform.

Day 16

*On that day all the fountains of the great deep were **broken up**, and the windows of heaven **were opened**.*

Heed the Warning!

The *fountains of the great deep* are, about, to be **broken up**, once again. And, God is *opening the windows of heaven*, for a **great downpour**. His **great outpouring** is poised, on the brink of Heaven—readying, to happen!

The **warning** has been sounded, all over the land. Preaching has gone forth, sounding the **alarm**! The world is looking on, as God's servants, busily, scurry about *erecting something*—they are not sure what! They, just, know they, too, are readying, for something—**BIG**!

At God's direction and with God's floor plan in hand, His servants are *erecting something* that will *house the souls of men*, when God's great outpouring begins. Whether you are INSIDE or OUTSIDE, of this *Spirit-prepared edifice*, will determine whether this outpouring will be one of **great judgment** or **great blessing**.

Once before, this scenario took place, in a wicked land called Egypt—symbolic of the world. Egypt housed and imprisoned God's Children, refusing to let them go. God *warned*, first, thereby giving opportunity, even, for His enemies to *take shelter*, if they *would*.

They were *warned* to **GET INSIDE** or be destroyed, along, with servants, livestock and crops, and whatever, else, remained **OUTSIDE**. If they *believed*, by bringing everyone and everything inside, they would be **spared**! But, if they *refused*, they would **die**![1]

Genesis 7:11 NKJ

What a picture of God's **warning** for mankind, today! The Israelites were *safe*, because they were in a *protective place*, called Goshen.

Goshen refers to *the place of the sun*. It means **approaching** and **drawing near.**[2] How appropriate, to the spiritual significance, of what God is teaching us. To survive the coming judgment, God is **warning the world and His Church:**

> *"Draw near. Approach Me, by means of my Son. Come into my Sanctuary. Close the door, and, there, sanctuary with Me!"*

In this place, you will be **safe** and **secure** from the wrath and judgment that is to come.

Heed the warning,
so you'll be **safe;**

Don't spurn His love,
or, you will **chafe!**

Day 17

Deep calls to deep in the roar of your waterfalls; all your waves and breakers have swept over me.

Deep Calls to Deep

The flood began, as the **fountains of the great deep** were *broken up.* Great *earthquakes* and *volcanic eruptions* happened, simultaneously, in numerous places.[1]

As the earth filled with water, the seismic activity sent *massive waves* surging, across the earth. This all brought about **great changes on the earth's surface,** such as the *Grand Canyon.*

As God is readying to unleash another **great outpouring,** from the open windows of Heaven, a **River** is beginning to flow on earth. The activity, of this *Great River,* is etching out **a Grand Canyon in God's people.**

Just, as rivers flow through channels, so **God is forming channels in His Children,** through whom this River must flow. Jesus foretold:[2]

> *"Whoever believes in Me, as the Scripture has said, **streams of living water will flow from within him."***

This River is **living**. Unlike the great flood in Genesis, wherever this River goes, **Life results,** not death![3] The reason is: the *Source* of this River is the *Holy Spirit.*

PSALM 42:7

Psalm 107:20 speaks of the Life-giving power of the Word:

"He sent His Word and healed them, and delivered them from their destructions."[4]

Full salvation, for spirit, body, and soul, in the form of great healings, deliverances, and miracles, will flow out of this River. As God sends forth His Word to heal, that Word will go into the **deep recesses** of man's spirit and begin to **break up** the great depths. The fountains, within, will, then, be released as rivers of **life-giving waters.**

The Holy Spirit is speaking to the **deep recesses** *within* man, as He *reveals* the things God has, *lovingly, prepared* for him:[5]

*"But God has revealed them to us through His Spirit. For the Spirit searches all things, yes, the **deep things of God.**"*

> The Spirit is calling
> **to deep within man,**
> while etching a channel,
> as fast as He can.
>
> A flood is coming
> as fountains break up,
> releasing visions of
> **God-prepared stuff!**

Day 18

For the earth will be full of the knowledge of the LORD as the waters cover the sea. In that day the Root of Jesse will stand as a banner for the peoples; the Nations will rally to Him, and His place of rest will be glorious.

A Deluge of Glory

As **sin has abounded,** so must **Grace, the more, abound.**[1] *Sin* abounded *in the days of Noah,* so *Grace* must abound, in these *latter days.* For, God has promised His Glory shall cover the earth.

Sin covered the world of Noah's day, followed by **a deluge of water.** Even so, **a deluge of Glory** is coming, which will fill the whole earth.

The *massive flood* **matched** the *wickedness,* which was great. Just so, Isaiah 59:19 assures, the Spirit of the LORD will, more than, **match** whatever the enemy may pull:[2]

> *"When the enemy comes in, like a flood the Spirit of the LORD will lift up a standard against him."*

Noah **prepared** an ark. to the saving of his household. Jesus, too, is **preparing** a place, to gather His household, which the Spirit of Glory longs to reveal:[3]

> *"No eye has seen, no ear has heard, no mind has conceived what God has **prepared** for those who love Him—but God has **revealed** it to us by His Spirit. The Spirit searches all things, even the **deep** things of God."*

ISAIAH 11:9 & 10

The Glory of God, revealed in the Son,[4] must, now, be revealed in His Bride.[5] She is going through a *preparation time,* to become a Glorious Church, without spot or wrinkle.[6] John said:[7]

> *"I saw the Holy City, the New Jerusalem, coming down out of Heaven from God, **prepared** as a Bride beautifully dressed for her husband."*

The worm emerges from its cocoon, transformed. If the newly, formed butterfly remains on the ground, it will be *vulnerable* to the smallest of predators, such as ants or spiders. Therefore, it *must* **take to the sky!** There, it will be *out of reach* and *elusive* to its would-be enemies.

The Church, as it is being transformed, faces a hostile world. She, too, *must* **take to the skies,** to survive. One day, she will be caught up to the place *prepared* by her Bridegroom: a **prepared Bride** for a **prepared place!**

But, until then, she must *stay elusive* and *out of reach* of her enemies, by **soaring in the Spirit.**

Take to the skies
and stay alive,
till Jesus comes
in the by-and-by!

Day 19

*The waters increased and **lifted up the ark**, and it rose high above the earth.*

The Great Divide

Jesus took the disciples onto the Sea of Galilee, to **separate** them from some things. God took the nation of Israel through the Red Sea, to **separate** them from some *Egyptian stuff.* Those, who refused to **let go,** died.

God took the three Hebrew children through the fire and **loosed** them from their bondages. God took Noah through a flood and **separated** him, from the *old world.*

God is taking His Church into **deep waters,** to *purify* and *separate* Her from stuff, too—stuff pertaining to the flesh and the world! He may, even, separate us from that most *dear*—as our Isaac. Martha lost that most *dear* to her, when Jesus let Lazarus die.

The floodwaters were an **ocean of judgment** to the wicked, but an **ocean of love,** for Noah. The same waters *drowned* them that *lifted* him to **greater heights**. God's love *lifted him* out of the angry waves, as goes the song, "Love Lifted Me." He was *lifted on wings of love*—like an eagle carrying her young.

The Redeemer speaks, if we will have ear to hear:[1]

> *"Oh, that you had heeded My commandments! Then your peace would have been **like a river**, and your righteousness like the waves of the sea."*

GENESIS 7:17 NKJ

God's Church can enjoy **rivers** of *Righteousness, Peace* and *Joy* in an **ocean of** *Love,* or be overcome by **floods of wickedness,** depending on her position.[2] Noah positioned himself in the ark, so that:

> *"As the water rose higher and higher above the ground, the boat floated safely upon it."*[3]

The LORD says to the *afflicted* and *tempest-tossed:*

> *"Just as in the time of Noah I swore that I would never again permit the waters of a flood to cover the earth and destroy its life, so now I swear that …My kindness shall not leave you. My promise of peace for you will never be broken…I will rebuild you…"*[4]

Let go of whatever
stands in the way,
of God's Holy Spirit
having full sway.

Let **deep rivers** of Peace,
with fullness of Joy,
lift up *your soul*
and unto Him **buoy!**

Day 20

*And the earth was without form, and void; and darkness was upon the face of the deep. And the Spirit of God **moved** upon the face of the waters.*

RESTORED BEAUTY

The Spirit **hovered** over the face of the waters, in the beginning of creation.[1] The idea behind hovering is a *sweeping, fluttering* or *shaking motion.*[2] One source infers that the Spirit was **dancing** over the waters.

The Spirit *danced on* the *face of the deep,* which was *waste* and *void,* just, as the ark **danced** on the flood:

> *"The waters prevailed and greatly increased on the earth, and the ark **moved about** on the surface of the waters."*[3]

The ark *danced on top* of all that corruption beneath, as it *rode above* the sea of judgment. The righteous, too, will **ride high** on the Spirit of the Lord, as He causes His Bride to **dance** upon Her circumstances, atop corruption and judgment that lie beneath her feet.

The DAY of the LORD, in which we live, will bring His *judgment* upon wickedness, along with *deliverance* and *restoration* of the righteous, as we, once again, witness a **moving of the Spirit** of God. David prophesied of this day:

> *"You have turned for me my mourning into **dancing.**"*[4]

Genesis 1:2 KJV

Isaiah, also, *prophesied* of this day, saying:

> *"The Spirit of the Lord GOD is **upon me**... to comfort all who mourn... in Zion, to give them **beauty for ashes,** the oil of joy for mourning, the garment of praise for the spirit of heaviness...."*[5]

Noah was **moved** by Godly fear, in preparing an ark.[6] Once again, the Spirit of the Lord is **moving upon His Church,** to bring **order out of chaos,** as He *restrains the flood* of wickedness:

> *"When the enemy comes in like a flood, the Spirit of the LORD will **lift up a standard** against him."*[7]

He is **beautifying** His Church, His crowning new-creation, just, as He *restored beauty* to His first creation.

God is **restoring the
Church** He has birthed;
just, as His Spirit
restored beauty to earth;

Ashes to beauty,
the joy of new wine:
all are **the work**
of His Spirit Divine!

Day 21

*For forty days the flood kept coming on the earth, and as the waters increased they **lifted the ark high above** the earth.*

A FIXED FOCUS

When things get, **too, corrupt**—there is, *only, one place* to go! With nothing, but *corruption*, all around him, Noah had to **pull into God**.

If corruption erupts, like sea billows, all around you: **Get to the Ark!** There, you will find *solace* and *peace*. There, Jesus can *speak*— **"Peace be still!"***[1]*

Once, Noah *knew* **THE ARK**: He could *build* one. He got the *pattern* for the ark, from **THE ARK**.*[2]* Having *built* the ark, Noah could *be one:* a place of *solace* and *comfort,* as reflected by his name.*[3]*

There is *no rest* for the wicked.*[4]* **REST** resides, only, within THE ARK: **Jesus.** When *resting in Him,* we can be *restful,* in the midst of great wickedness, as we *ride on top* of the storm. THE ARK will cause us to *rise above* the sea of corruption.

By faith, Peter *walked upon the water.* By faith, I must *walk upon whatever it is that would sweep me under.* Note, it was, only, as Peter walked *focused upon* and *moving toward* Jesus, that he could **walk on top!***[5]*

Stay focused on Jesus, through His Word, and you, too, will be able to **walk above:**

GENESIS 7:17

"Let us fix our eyes on Jesus, the author and perfecter of our faith, who for the joy set before Him endured the cross, scorning its shame, and sat down at the right hand of the Throne of God. Consider Him who endured such opposition from sinful men, so that you will not grow weary and lose heart."

Hebrews 12:2 & 3

This passage is saying: **"Have eyes for no one, but Jesus!"** Consider Him, by looking away from everything, else, as you look, with undivided attention.

Fix your gaze, so as, not to be distracted, in the least. It will take this kind of **fixed focus,** if you are to **walk on top!**

To **walk atop**
all that slop
the world has mixed:

My gaze must **stay**
FIXED!

Day 22

Then he sent out a raven, which kept going to and fro until the waters had dried up from the earth.

A Ravenous Raven

The raven is **not a relational bird**. There is no indication of a relationship between Noah and the raven. Noah never used the terms **to himself** or **from himself** with the raven, as with the dove.

Neither did Noah use gender pronouns, when referring to the raven. The raven was merely an "**it**," whereas, the dove was referred to as **she** and **her**.

Scripture, simply, says, "Then he sent out a raven." It went out, never to return. I John 2:19 states:[1]

> "*They went out from us, but they were not of us; for if they had been of us, they would have continued with us; but they went out that they might be made manifest, that none of them were of us.*"

The nature of the raven was *manifested,* when it failed to return. John warns the Church, in the last days, some will come among us, who are not of us. Because they are **not of us**, they will **not continue with us**.

A raven is **a dirty bird**.[2] *Raven* and **ravenous** are related words, which describe one, whose desires or appetites **cannot be satisfied**. They are, overly, eager to **gratify** their **huge, fleshly appetites**. As *coveters,* they live on their prey.[3]

Genesis 8:6 & 7 NKJ

We, easily, see how the raven **pictures the, fleshly, nature of man.** When Noah sent out this flesh eating bird, time passed, as it, *ravenously, feasted* on flesh.

God warns, "Do not trust in the arm of the flesh." Do not send out the **flesh,** to get God's message.[4] The *lower nature* cannot receive or give Godly direction.[5]

The flesh is good at *benefiting* from that which costs it *nothing,* but costs others *everything.* It doesn't mind *feeding on dead things.*

The raven went **to and fro,** indicating it was *restless.* The dove could find **no rest** in the world, either, so it **sought the resting place.** *Restless* and *unsatisfied,* the flesh, as the raven, will continue in its carnage, for it knows nothing of **rest within THE ARK.**

The world cannot give
you **eternal rest;**
but, every vestige of life,
from you will **wrest!**

It's a "dog, eat dog" world;
so, don't, even, think:
"I'll give it a whirl."
Or, you'll, **surely, sink!**

Day 23

But the dove found no rest for the sole of her foot, and she returned unto him into the ark; for the waters were on the face of the whole earth. Then he put forth his hand, and took her, and pulled her in unto him in the ark.

REST, DON'T WREST

The *raven* and *dove* represent the contrasting **natures** and **appetites,** of the fleshly or carnal man, and that of the spiritual man: one *feeds* at the **table of devils** (the raven), while the other *partakes* of the **Lord's table.** [1]

Seeing, only, *corruption, decay* and *death* through dove's eyes, the dove **returned** to the hand of the one, who sent her forth. [2] She **returned,** unto her *ark of safety.* The ark was:

- A **Protective Place,**
- A **Hiding Place,**
- A **Shelter** from the storm.

Noah means *rest, comfort* or *comforter.* [3] From within the ark, Noah **put forth his hand** and **took the dove** and **pulled her in, unto himself,** into a *place of comfort.* The dove could not find rest out there, over the earth, so she **returned** to the **place of rest,** *within the ark.*

Our rest and inheritance is, also, **within our Ark, Christ Jesus.** Jesus gave this invitation, in Matthew 11:28:

> *"Come to Me, all you who are weary and burdened and I will give you rest."*

Genesis 8:9 KJV

Jesus said, "Come to Me, personally." He gives us this **rest,** as we

- **Come** to Him
- **Learn** of Him
- **Partake** of Him, and
- **Eat at His table.**

There, we'll find **comfort for our souls!**

If **pulled** by the world,
heavy burdens you'll **wrest;**

Be **pulled** into Jesus:
your **Haven of Rest!**

Day 24

*Blessed be the God and Father of our Lord Jesus Christ, who according to His abundant mercy has begotten us again to a living hope through the resurrection of Jesus Christ from the dead, **to an inheritance incorruptible** and **undefiled**, and that **does not fade away, reserved in heaven** for you.*

INHERIT INCORRUPTION

God's inheritance, **reserved in Heaven,** will not be found *in corruption,* as illustrated by the dove. Noah sent out the *raven,* then, the *dove.[1]* These two birds are *two, contrasting natures*:

- that of the **old natural man** in Adam, represented by the *raven;* and
- that of the **new nature** from God, represented by the *dove.*

The LORD told Joshua:[2]

> *"Every place that the sole of your foot shall tread upon, that have I given unto you."*

Every place that Joshua *walked* was to be his inheritance. But, this dove could not find a place of *rest* or *inheritance,* for its feet.[3] The waters, still, covered the earth, indicating that death and corruption, still, lay upon the face of the waters. Therefore, the dove, true to its nature, **returned to the ark.**

Representative of the sin-corrupted nature, the raven, instead, lighted upon and **fed on,** *all, that decaying flesh.* Similarly, the old sinful nature of man *feeds upon the corruption of this world,* satisfying its appetite for evil.

54

I Peter 1:3 & 4 NKJ

Ephesians 4:19 says of such:

> "*Who, being past feeling, have given themselves over to lewd-*
> *ness, to work all uncleanness with greediness.*"[4]

If *dead,* you are **past feeling**. And, these *spiritually, dead folk,* of
Ephesians 4, were *past feeling,* in doing evil. Their old natures were
corrupted by deceitful desires.[5]

God does not will his children to inherit *death* and *corruption.*
Therefore, we must become a new creation, fashioned after God's
nature, which is characterized by *righteousness and true holiness.*

If we *walk*
IN CORRUPTION,
we cannot *inherit*
INCORRUPTION!

Day 25

*But the **dove could find no place to set its feet** because there was water over all the surface of the earth; so **it returned to Noah in the ark**. He reached out his hand and took the dove and brought it back to himself in the ark.*

Quiet Brooks Beside Still Waters

We have all, probably, seen children's storybooks, picturing Noah, with a dove on His shoulder. Very likely, the dove perched there, but Scripture does not tell us so. It, just, says Noah **drew her** into the ark, **to himself**.[1] The personal pronouns, *she* and *her*, are used to refer to the dove.

Genesis 8:8 says, Noah "sent out **from himself** a dove."[2] Scripture speaks of the dove, in relation to Noah, as though the dove abode with him. A relationship, very likely, developed between the two.

Every created thing on that ark had an allotted place. Yet, the dove chose to be **closest to its master**. How like the beloved John and Mary, sister of Martha, who sought to be **near their Master**.

David declares:

> *"The Lord Himself is my inheritance, my prize. He is my food and drink, my highest joy! He guards all that is mine."*
>
> *Psalm 16:5 LB*

When Noah, first, sent out the dove, there was neither *inheritance* nor *resting place*, for the sole of her feet. So, **she returned, to inherit a place, where her feet could rest**—the strong hand of Noah.

GENESIS 8:9

The dove could find no food or drink, to satisfy her thirst and hunger, *outside* the ark. The waters over the earth were tainted with carnage. So, she took **shelter, within the ark,** amply supplied with pure, clean water.

The dove chose to be fed by the hand of Noah and to drink from pure cisterns. May we, too, choose to eat from the hand of our God, Who gives, each day, *our daily bread,* in ample supply.[3]

Speaking of her Beloved, the Shulamite said:[4]

"His eyes are like doves beside the water brooks, deep and quiet."

Doves need the **deep, quiet** water brooks, as do His sheep, whom the Beloved Shepherd is seen leading, beside **still** waters.[5]

Lord, I'm **leaning**
on your breast,
where there is **solace**
and **sweet rest**.

All my need,
You **amply supply**.
So, in You, I will **abide!**

Day 26

*His eyes are like doves beside the water brooks, **deep** and **quiet**.*

Pools of Deep Love

In our Savior's eyes, there are **deep pools** of *love* for His dove, His Bride. The Shepherd knocks at the Shulamite's door and says:

> *"Open for me, my sister, my darling, my dove, my flawless one. My head is drenched with dew, my hair with the dampness of the night."*

> *Song of Solomon 5:2*

Notice how he addressed her:

- My sister
- My darling
- My dove
- My flawless one

Our Lord is coming for His Bride, a chaste virgin, that is:[1]

- Glorious
- Having no spot
- Having no wrinkle
- Holy
- Without blemish

I cannot help, but think of the Bride of Christ, as I consider this dove, who *refused to be defiled*. Instead, **she sought solace and rest with her master.**

Song of Solomon 5:12 LB

Envision, meeting your Shepherd, and being drawn into His Presence. As you stand face to face, **He looks deep into your eyes, with eyes full of love.**

You look into His, only, to discover they are so **deep,** you have become lost in them. Their depths are **fathomless,** like an ocean without bottom. As you drink of His love, it is so **immeasurable,** that you're unable to contain it. Yet, in those eyes, there is a **peace** *that brings a sense of* **quiet, loving acceptance** *to your soul.* He knows everything about you, yet, intensely loves you.

The Shepherd is calling at the door of His Bride's heart, today, *seeking entry.* If you will *open* **your heart to Him,** He will come in and commune with you, face to face. May the cry and response of your heart be:[2]

> *"As the deer pants after the water brooks, so* **pants** *my soul for You, O God, My soul* **thirsts** *for God, for the living God."*

Lord, may my *heart,*
never, from Your love, **turn;**

but like a *hart,*
for You, **ever yearn.**

Day 27

*The water had **dried up** from the earth. Noah then removed the covering from the ark and saw that the surface of the ground was **dry**.*

SACRIFICIAL PRAISE

It must have been a very **dramatic thing,** for Noah and his family to step from the ark, to a world swept clean of *wickedness,* even *life—* onto **dry land,** left *desolate, parched, ruined* and *wasted* by the flood.[1]

Israel had a very **dramatic experience,** as they left Egypt and crossed the Red Sea, on **dry land.** *Dry,* in this case, means *dry, withered, disappointed, ashamed,* or *confused.*[2]

Salvation is a very **dramatic experience,** too, often referred to as *conversion,* in which, we leave one realm of life, to enter another. Our past is *washed away,* as pictured by both Noah's and Israel's experiences.

The past must be *forgotten.* We cannot cling to *past memories* and enter our Promise Land. That would be to live, bodily, in one world, while in memory, another. **The past is** *past,* to which we can, never, return.

We will face **dry times,** as we await fulfillment of God's promises. The Lord may, even, lead through some *parched* and *desolate wastelands.*

The number 40 refers to a time of testing.[3] Noah, having *endured* the 40-day rains, then, awaited *dry land.*[4] Israel *endured* a 40-year wilderness, then, awaited entry to the Promised Land. Enduring such times, even *confusion* and *disappointment,* readies us for our Promised Land.

GENESIS 8:13

Noah *waited* for the waters to **recede** and dry land to **appear.** As we wait, God causes *old things of the past* to **recede** in our lives and *new things* to **appear. Wait** means the same as *expectation, hope,* or *trust,* as one awaiting God's mercy, salvation or rescue.[5]

Once converted, we must face the desolate and parched wastelands and the voids in our lives, left by past sin. The past is gone, but not all its *effects* disappear, at once. This can cause hope to *wither* and faith to give way to *confusion, shame* and *disappointment.* Then is when we need to build an altar and offer up a **sacrifice of praise and worship** to our God.[6]

When life seems *dry*
and *void of life,*

offer to God
your *sweet-sacrifice*

of **praise** and **worship,**
with up-lifted hands,

till on solid ground
you, once again, stand.

Day 28

*Then **Noah built an altar to the LORD** and, taking some of all the clean animals and clean birds, he sacrificed burnt offerings on it.*

A Contrasting Life

After everything on the earth had been destroyed, except those in the ark, the **first thing Noah did,** upon exiting the ark, was to **build an altar** to *sacrifice clean animals to God.*

> *"And Jehovah was **pleased** with the sacrifice and **smelled the delicious odor** and said, 'I will never do it again: …curse the earth.'"*

> *Genesis 8:21 LB*

Do you think that Father God might have **smelled the sweet-smelling sacrifice of His Son,** on that special day, *as Noah offered up those sacrificial animals?* You do not have to offer up animals, today, like Noah, because Jesus was your sin offering.

Through means of that offering, God can, also, **find favor** in you, though others, around you, continue in much wickedness. Though the directions of their lives are, only, towards evil, His Grace will enable you to bring much **pleasure** to Him, *as you walk with God.*

Noah's life was a **contrast** to those living in his day, because he **chose** to *walk with God.* We will either *walk with God* or *walk with the wicked* of this world. We cannot do both. We are admonished, to be a **contrast:**

Genesis 8:20

"Let there be no sex sin, impurity or greed, among you. Let no one be able to accuse you of any such thing. Dirty stories, foul talk and coarse jokes—are not for you."

Ephesians 5:3 & 4 LB

This passage, in Ephesians, goes on to tell you what you are to do, when others around you *practice* these things and, then, *brag* about it:

"Don't be fooled by those who try to excuse these sins, for the terrible wrath of God is upon all those who do them. Don't even associate with such people. For though once your heart was full of darkness, now it is full of light from the Lord, and your behavior should show it!"

Ephesians 5:6–8 LB

Your life must **CONTRAST,**
not **CONFORM,**
to the world's walk!!

Day 29

In this world you will have trouble. But take heart! ***I have overcome the world.***

ESCAPING CORRUPTION

Noah **overcame** the world, in his day. The people of Noah's day didn't know God. They rejected His Word, by ignoring the preaching of Noah—both by life and his words. Because of this, they were condemned, whereas **Noah became heir to righteousness.**[1]

Noah *remained righteous,* despite living in a sea of corruption. He **rose above that corruption,** around him, even in the midst of God's judgment, because he was *hidden in the ark of God's Presence.*

Through Jesus, our Ark, we can **overcome.** We can experience His peace, *in the midst of our troubled and corrupt world.* We can experience His Presence, also, as we tell others, in the world, of Him.

We have been given, exceedingly, great and precious *promises,* so that, sharing in God's divine nature, we **shall escape the corruption** that is in the world, arising through lust or passion.[2] Just, as God gave Noah *promise* of *protection* and *safety,* through his obedience, so are we given this *promise* and *assurance* of His Presence, as we obey:

JOHN 16:33

"...*As God has said: 'I will dwell in them and walk among them. I will be their God, and they will be my people.' Therefore, 'Come out from among them and be separate,' says the Lord. 'Do not touch what is unclean, and I will receive you. I will be a Father to you, and you will be my sons and daughters,' says the LORD Almighty. Therefore, **having these promises, beloved, let us cleanse ourselves from all filthiness of the flesh and spirit, perfecting holiness in the fear of God.***"*

2 Corinthians 6:16–18 & 17:1 NKJ

When we determine not to touch what is unclean and corrupt, and to cleanse ourselves from all filthiness of the flesh and spirit, our Comforter will **reach out** His hand, **take us** and **pull us unto Himself,** within the Ark, Christ Jesus.

Let Him pull you into the **Ark of His Presence!**

To **draw nigh**
is God's will;

So, **draw nigh:**
You will prevail!

Day 30

*I have told you all this so that you will have peace of heart and mind. Here on earth you will have many trials and sorrows; but **cheer up**, for I have overcome the world.*

CHEERFUL ENDURANCE

Jesus *warned* his disciples, on the eve of His crucifixion, that in this life, *hard times* are unavoidable. But, **they could have *peace, quietness and rest*** in Him.

This is the message of Noah: **In the ark,** was *comfort, quietness and rest,* while **outside, in the world,** was, only, *unrest.* "'There is no peace', says My God, 'for the wicked'"[1]

Jesus followed the warning with *encouragement:* **Cheer up!** He is not telling us to go down to the local bar and get some *cheer.* The world has a counterfeit they call happy hour. But, **the *real cheer* and,** *truly, happy hour* **comes from God.**

Cheer, basically, means to **take courage.**[2] How many have sat, sipping the world's cheer, trying to gather courage. But, it doesn't work. The disciples of Jesus could take courage, because Jesus **overcame** anything and everything they would, ever, face in life.

It took **courage,** for Israel *to enter the Promised Land,* so Joshua was told to **be of good courage.**[3] It took **courage,** for the disciples *to be faithful,* under great persecution. It took **courage,** for Noah *to build an ark.* And, it will take **courage,** for you *to overcome.*

Overcome means **to subdue.**[4] Israel had to **conquer** the enemy that occupied its inheritance. We, too, must **dispossess** every enemy, squatting on our inheritance, to **possess** all God has promised.

John 16:33 LB

This **courage** must consist of **endurance:**[5]

"For you have need of endurance, so that after you have done the will of God, you may receive the promise."

Endurance is **the capacity to** *bear up,* *under very difficult circumstances,* **with a hope that resists weariness and defeat.** "You have *need of endurance,"* Paul said. Therefore, he invites you to come, boldly, to the Throne of Grace and *get what you need.*[6]

This is not an *option. If you are to overcome* the squeezing and crushing, the pressures, the anguish and distress, Jesus called *tribulation,* it will take **courage** and **endurance.**[7]

I give you *Peace,*
cause I **overcame;**

Go in My *Strength*
and **you'll do the same!**

Day 31

*But the dove found no place to light, and returned to Noah, for the water was still too high. So Noah held out his hand and **drew the dove back into the boat.***

A Three-Fold Cord

The ark represents Jesus, our Ark of Safety. Noah, the *comforter,* represents the person and work of the Holy Spirit, who was sent to be *our Comforter.*

Noah **drew** the dove unto himself. Some versions say: "He **pulled** her unto himself."[1] **Drew** reflects the work of the Holy Spirit, in drawing saint and sinner. He must *draw* the lost, before they can be saved.[2] He is the One, who *pulls on* their conscience, in conviction of sin, of their need of a Savior, and of the coming judgment.[3]

The Holy Spirit *draws* the saint, ever, *closer* to Jesus, our abiding place. He invites us to *draw near,* as He, in turn, *draws closer* to us.[4]

The dove represents **three stages of the believer's life**. When the dove went out, it returned to Noah. The first stage, of our Christian walk, necessitates that we **draw near to Jesus** and *habitat with Him,* in His Presence. We must **possess Him**, not, just, as Savior, but *all aspects* of His Person and relationship to us.

Having come to **abide in Jesus**, we can, then, go on to **possess His Kingdom**. The dove reflects this, by its second exit from the ark. This time, she returned with an olive branch. It is God's good pleasure to give us the Kingdom.[5] Jesus instructed us to seek it and His Righteousness, first.[6] The Kingdom is characterized by *Righteousness, Peace,* and *Joy* in the Spirit.[7]

GENESIS 8:9 LB

We must, **first, possess Christ,** if we are to bring God's Kingdom to earth. We must **possess the Kingdom, inwardly,** by establishing Jesus' character and rule of peace, in our inner lives, before we can, ever, hope to establish it, **outwardly.** Next, is the third stage.

This time, when Noah sent out the dove, she *did not return.* As the first two conditions of maturity are met, the Holy Spirit (Noah) will release us out into the world, to **carry the Everlasting Gospel** to it. Only, then, can He **establish His ministry on the earth,** through us.

Another way of putting the three stages, in order, is:

- **Jesus** (intimacy)
- **others** (servant hood)
- **you** (ministry).

Put Jesus **first**
and you'll be blest!

Seek others **good,**
and you'll pass the test!

If you have learned,
"It's more blessed to give:"

for **Jesus** and **others,**
you'll **always,** then, **live!**

NOTES

Day 1

1 James Strong, *Strong's Exhaustive Concordance of the Bible (Christian Heritage Publishing Co. Inc., 1988),* based on the Hebrew entry #7843.

2 See Ephesians 2:1 & 2 in the King James Version.

Day 2

1 *Strong's,* based on the Hebrew entry #7451.

2 *Strong's,* based on the Hebrew entry #7489, the root word for #7451. The definition is from "Lexicon To The Old And New Testaments", edited by Spiros Zodhiates, *The Hebrew-Greek Key Study Bible, King James Version, (AMG Publishers, Chattanoga, TN).* The Lexicon entries correspond to Strong's numbering system.

3 Zodhiates, *Lexicon,* Hebrew entry #7451.

4 See Genesis 1:29 & 31.

5 See Genesis 6:5. Zodhiates, *Lexicon,* based on the Hebrew entry #2555.

6 Words based on definitions given in Zodhiates, *Lexicon,* Hebrew entry #2555 and its root #2554.

7 Definition based on *Strong's* Hebrew entry #7227 and its root # 7231. See, also *The Spirit Filled Life Bible, New King James, (Nelson Publishers), Word Wealth,* Psalm 31:19, *Strong's* #7227.

Day 3

1 See Genesis 6:12.

2 See Hebrews 11:7, New King James.

3 See Hebrews 1:1 & 2; 2:3.

Day 4

1 See Genesis 6:22.

2 See 2 Peter 3:9.

Day 5

1 See Genesis 6:8.

2 See Genesis 6:5, Living Bible.

3 See Genesis 6:6, New International Version.

Day 6

1 See Ephesians 5:2, New King James.
2 See Ephesians 4:32.
3 See Ephesians 5:2.
4 See Ephesians 5:8.
5 See Ephesians 5:15.
6 See Ephesians 2:10; 4:10.
7 See Ephesians 5:15.
8 See Ephesians 4:17, 22.

Day 7

1 See in New King James Version.
2 See John 8:32 & 36.

Day 8

1 The Spirit Life Bible, Word Wealth, Zechariah 12:10, Strong's #2580.
2 Ibid.
3 See Exodus 33:12, New King James.

Day 9

1 See Exodus 33:8.
2 See Hebrews 4:16 in New King James.

Day 10

1 See Hebrews 4:16.
2 See Ephesians 1:17.
3 See Luke 10:42 & John 12:3.
4 See Exodus 24:18; 33:11–13.
5 See John 1:9–17.
6 See Matthew 17:2 & 3.
7 See John 11:40 & I Peter 1:8.

Day 11

1 See John 6:8 & 9.
2 See Mark 6:34–41.
3 See Matthew 7:8 & Hebrews 4:12.

Day 12

1 Strong's, based on the Hebrew entry # 1613.

2 Strong's, based on the root Hebrew entry #3722. See, also, Zodhiates, Lexicon, entry # 3722. See John Davis, A Dictionary of the Bible, (The Westminister Press, Philadelphia, 1934), p. 613.

3 Strong's, based on the Hebrew entry #3724. See, also, Zodhiates, Lexicon, entry #3724.

4 Davis, A Dictionary of the Bible, p. 300.

5 The Spirit Filled Life Bible, Word Wealth, Numbers 15:25, Strong's #3722.

6 See John 14:2 & 3.

7 See Genesis 8:13 in New King James.

8 Strong's, based on the Hebrew entry #4377 & its root, #3680.

9 Zodhiates, Lexicon, entry # 3680.

Day 14

1 See Psalm 66:11 & 12.

Day 15

1 See Psalm 66:12 in King James Version.

2 See Psalm 66:12 in New King James.

3 See Psalm 23:5.

4 Strong's, based on the Hebrew entry #7310 & its root, #7301.

Day 16

1 See Exodus 9:18 & 19.

2 Judson Cornwall & Dr. Stelman Smith, The Exhaustive Dictionary of Bible Names, (Bridge–Logos Publishers, NJ), p. 93.

Day 17

1 The Spirit Filled Life Bible, Genesis 7:11 footnote & Word Wealth, Isaiah 43:2, Strong's #4325.

2 See John 7:38.

3 See Ezekiel 47:9.

4 See Psalm 107:20 in New King James.

5 See I Corinthians 2:10 in New King James.

Day 18

1 See Romans 5:20 in New King James.

2 See Isaiah 59:19 in New King James.

3 See I Corinthians 2:9–10.

4 See John 17:1–5, 22–24.

5 See Romans 8:18 & Revelation 21:9–11.

6 See Ephesians 6:27.

7 See Revelation 21:2.

Day 19

1 See Isaiah 48:18 in New King James.

2 See Romans 14:17.

3 See Genesis 7:18 in Living Bible.

4 See Isaiah 54:9–11 in Living Bible.

Day 20

1 See Genesis 1:2 in New King James and New International Version.

2 The Spirit Filled Life Bible, Genesis 1:2 footnote.

3 See Genesis 7:18 in New King James.

4 See Psalm 30:11 in New King James.

5 See Isaiah 61:1–3 in New King James.

6 See Hebrews 11:7 in King James Version.

7 See Isaiah 59:19 in New King James.

Day 21

1 See Mark 4:39 in New King James.

2 See Genesis 6:14–16.

3 The Spirit Filled Bible, Word Wealth, Exodus 33:14, Strong's #5117 & Isaiah 28:12, Strong's #4496.

4 See Isaiah 48:22. See, also, Strong's, based on Hebrew entry #7965, which can be translated peace & rest. See Zodhiates, Lexicon, entry # 7965 & entry #7999.

5 See Matthew 14:28–30.

Day 22

1 See I John 2:19 in New King James.

2 See Leviticus 11:13–15 & Deuteronomy 14:11–14.

3 Merriam–Webster, Webster's Seventh New Collegiate Dictionary, (G. & C. Merriam Co., 1969), p. 711.

4 See Jeremiah 17:5.

5 See 1 Corinthians 2:14.

Day 23

1 See 1 Corinthians 10:21.
2 See Song of Solomon 5:12.
3 Cornwall & Smith, *The Exhaustive Dictionary of Bible Names*, p. 194.

Day 24

1 See Genesis 8:7 & 8.
2 See Joshua 1:3 in King James Version.
3 See Genesis 8:9 in New King James.
4 See Ephesians 4:19 in New King James.
5 See Ephesians 4:22.

Day 25

1 See Genesis 8:9 in New King James.
2 See Genesis 8:8.
3 See Matthew 6:11.
4 See Song of Solomon 5:12 in Living Bible.
5 See Psalm 23:2.

Day 26

1 See 2 Corinthians 11:2 & Ephesians 5:27.
2 See Psalm 42:1 & 2 in New King James.

Day 27

1 Strong's, based on Hebrew entry #2720 & entry #2724. Zodhiates, Lexicon, entry #2720.
2 Strong's, based on Hebrew entry #3004 & its root, entry #3001.
3 Ed Vallowe, Biblical Mathematics, (Ed. Vallowe Evangelistic Association, Georgia, 1988), p. 173.
4 See Genesis 7:4 & 12.
5 See Genesis 8:12. See, also, *The Spirit Filled Life Bible, Word Wealth, Micah 7:7, Strong's #3176*.
6 See Genesis 8:20.

Day 29

1 See Hebrews 11:7.
2 See 2 Peter 1:3 & 4.

Day 30

1 See Isaiah 48:22.

2 Strong's, based on the Greek entry #2293.

3 See Joshua 1:7 & 9. See, also, The Spirit Filled Life Bible, Word Wealth, Joshua 1:9, Strong's #2388.

4 Strong's, based on the Greek entry #3528 & its root, # 3529.

5 Strong's, based on Greek entry # 5278. See, also, The Spirit Filled Life Bible, Word Wealth, Hebrews 10:36, Strong's #5281 & Matthew 24:13, Strong's #5278 & 2 Thessalonians 1:4, Strong's #430.

6 See Hebrews 4:16.

7 The Spirit Filled Life Bible, Word Wealth, John 16:33, Strong's #2347.

Day 31

1 See Genesis 8:9 in King James Version.

2 See John 6:44.

3 See John 16:8.

4 See James 4:8.

5 See Luke 12:32

6 See Matthew 6:33.

7 See Romans 14:17.

Addendum

If you have never made covenant with God and come into an intimate relationship with Him, you may do so, **RIGHT NOW!** It is much like taking the marriage vows, when you pledge your life to the one you love.

You, first, must admit that you have sinned. The Bible says your sins have separated you from God (Isaiah 59:1, 2). Therefore, to experience a relationship with God, your sins must be forgiven.

The Bible, further, explains that we are all born, spiritually, dead (Ephesians 2:1). Therefore, you need spiritual **LIFE**. The Bible calls this **Eternal Life** (John 10:28). It is the God-kind of Life, which never ends. It is, also, a quality kind of Life, that is God's very own, full of joy, peace, and love (Galations 5:22–23).

To give us His Life, God had to send a substitute, in our place, to take the judgment for our sins; for the wages, or payment due sin, is **DEATH** (Romans 6:23). God told Adam, the day he sinned, he would, surely, die. That **DEATH** *passed on* to Cain and on down, through the generations, to every person, born into this world.

The **GOOD NEWS** is: Jesus was our substitute. He was the **PERFECT** Son of God, without sin. He was in Eternity with Father God, before the world began. Jesus was, and is, very God (John 1:1–3). He chose to become the baby in the manger, so He could have a body, with which to go to the cross, for you and me (Hebrews 10:5).

The Bible, further, tells us, Jesus bore our sins and iniquities (Isaiah 53:4–5; 2 Corinthians 5:21). That means He not, only, paid the punishment for all the sins you, ever, committed, so you could be forgiven. But, He, also, took your sinful nature, or you, to the cross with Him, so you could be set free, from that within, which causes you to sin.

When one gets married, each gives up all rights to an independent life, agreeing to **SHARE LIFE** in a way that brings each, into agreement or **oneness** of relationship, in everything. All is done in **UNION** with the one, to whom each pledges his or her life and love to—that is marriage! That is true covenant!

To experience this **ONENESS**, in covenant with God, one must be willing to give up being independent, and the "me, me, me" attitude, of getting one's own way. If you are ready to surrender to God, in this way, making Him the center and the one in control of your life, to live your life in union with Him, pledging your love and desire, only, to Him, as a wife would her husband, then repeat a simple prayer, pledging your vows.

But, like a true husband in love, God will not take advantage of your commitment to Him, by returning evil. The Bible says that what God has in mind for you is good, full of peace, blessing, and freedom, not evil (Jeremiah 29:11).

Pray:

God, I have sinned, against You. I deserve death and separation from You. But, I believe You so loved me, that You sent Jesus, to die for me. Because of the death He died and the blood He shed, I can be forgiven and set free from sin, and who I was, while in rebellion, against You. Right, now, I receive Jesus, as my Savior and Lord. Much like a marriage on earth, I pledge You my love and obedience. I surrender my will to You, realizing my life is no longer mine.

In return, I receive forgiveness for my sins (past, present, and future). I receive Eternal Life. And, I come into covenant relationship, with You, meaning we will, now, walk in intimate fellowship. I do not, fully, understand all about this, but I know, as I come to know You, intimately, I will grow and will become one with You, more, every day. Therefore, I will spend time, **ALONE, WITH YOU**—*talking to You in prayer, listening to You, hearing Your voice in Your Word (the Bible), so I might know what You want me to do and be like, seeking to please, only, You. I pledge my love to You, alone, meaning I will cleave to You and not to the world, its attractions and, even, close friends. Here is my heart, take it and make it Your own and Your home. Thank You for giving Yourself for me and to me, that I might live with You, forever. amen!*

Having prayed this prayer, you have, just, entered into an eternal contract, or covenant of promise, with God. Be aware of this—you, now, have an enemy, even, more committed to your destruction. Like an old "flame" or close friend, with whom you have "gone out," he will try to persuade you to return. He does not give up, easily. How successful you are in walking, victoriously, in this new life and intimate relationship with God, will be determined by how much you love Him, how *completely* you submit your will and desires to Him, and how *devotedly* you seek and cleave, only, to Him.

Just, as there are witnesses, when you get married, so this marriage contract needs witnesses. Romans 10:9 says we are to **CONFESS** with our mouth, Jesus, as our Lord. In other words, **TELL SOMEBODY** your decision. Jesus promised that, if we confess Him **BEFORE MEN,** He will confess us **BEFORE HIS FATHER,** in Heaven.

Next, determine to be *faithful* to the Lord and His church. Hebrews 10:25 emphasizes the importance of this, in the days in which we are living: "Let us not *neglect* our church meetings, as some people do, but encourage and *warn* each other, especially, now that the day of His coming back, again, is drawing near" (LB). Therefore, the most, important thing you can do, along with those things, already, mentioned, is find the church, where God would have you attend, and be faithful. This will be your **own, spiritual family,** where you are fed, nurtured and cared for, as you grow. You cannot be strong, or victorious, without it. Do it, today!

God bless you.

www.ingramcontent.com/pod-product-compliance
Lightning Source LLC
Chambersburg PA
CBHW060140050426
42448CB00010B/2228